Jonah
runs away

Story by Penny Frank
Illustrated by Tony Morris

Guideposts
30

CARMEL • NEW YORK 10512

The Bible tells us
how God chose the nation of Israel to
be his special people. He made them a
promise that he would always love
and care for them. But they must
obey him.

God often sent special prophets to
give his messages to the people. This
story is about the prophet Jonah. You
can find his story in the part of the
Bible which has his name.

Copyright © 1987 Lion Publishing

Published by
Lion Publishing plc
Icknield Way, Tring, Herts, England
Lion Publishing Corporation
1705 Hubbard Avenue, Batavia,
Illinois 60510, USA
Albatross Books Pty Ltd
PO Box 320, Sutherland, NSW 2232, Australia

First edition 1987
Reprinted 1987

Printed and bound in Hong Kong by Mandarin Offset
This Guideposts edition is published by special arrangement with Lion Publishing

**British Library Cataloguing in
Publication Data**

Frank, Penny
Jonah runs away.—(The Lion Story
Bible; 30)
1. Jonah—Juvenile literature
I. Title   II. Morris, Tony, *1938 Aug 2 –*
224'.920924   BS580.J55

**Library of Congress Cataloging-in-
Publication Data**

Frank, Penny.
Jonah runs away.
(The Lion Story Bible; 30)
1. Jonah (Biblical prophet)—Juvenile
literature. [1. Jonah (Biblical prophet)
2. Bible stories—O.T.] I. Morris, Tony,
ill. II. Title. III. Series: Frank, Penny.
Lion Story Bible; 30.
BS580.J33F73 1987   224'.9209505
86-15313

Once upon a time there lived a man
called Jonah. He was a prophet. God
had specially chosen him to take
messages to his people.

But Jonah did not always do as God
said.

One day God said, 'Jonah, I want you to
go to Nineveh. It's an enormous city. It's
full of people who do bad things. You
must tell them that if they go on like
this I will destroy them.'

The people in Nineveh were enemies of God's people. Jonah wanted God to destroy them. But he did not want to go to Nineveh.

'I know what will happen,' he thought to himself. 'It's happened before! If I go to Nineveh with that message the people will be afraid. They will tell God they are sorry and, because he is a loving God, he will forgive them. I would much rather he punished them.'

So Jonah ran the other way, away from Nineveh.

Jonah wanted to get away from God —
and from Nineveh. So he went down to
the sea and asked for a ride in a boat.

When the boat had started on its
journey, Jonah felt better.

'God hasn't spoken to me while I've
been on the boat, so I must have left
him behind,' thought Jonah. 'And I'm
certainly going away from Nineveh.'

But after a little while a terrible storm began. The boat went up and down on the enormous waves. The wind blew it in the wrong direction. The sailors were frightened. They thought they would all be drowned.

But Jonah got onto his bunk and went to sleep.

'When I wake up the storm will have stopped,' he thought.

Jonah slept, but only for a little while. Then the ship's captain came to wake him up.

'What are you doing, asleep?' he asked. 'We're all going to be drowned. Don't you have a god to pray to?'

Then Jonah saw how silly he had been.
    'It's all my fault,' he said. 'My God
has sent this storm to stop me running
away from him. If you throw me into
the sea, the storm will stop.'

The captain was afraid. He did not want Jonah to drown. But Jonah knew it was the only way to stop the storm.

So in the end they threw Jonah over the side, into the water. The storm stopped at once.

Then the captain and the other men said, 'This God of Jonah's must be very powerful if even the storm obeys him.'

They didn't know that God had sent an enormous fish to swallow Jonah.

Jonah was very frightened. It was slimy and dark inside the fish.

'Help me,' he shouted to God. 'I can see how stupid I've been. You are a great God and I should be obeying you.'

After three days, the fish spat Jonah out onto some sand. Then it swam away, feeling much better.

'Now,' God said to Jonah, 'please stop being silly. Go to Nineveh, as I told you.'

So Jonah set off for Nineveh. He could still remember what God had told him to say.

Jonah told the people in Nineveh that God was angry about the things they did. He said that God would punish them if they did not change.

The people believed him. They told God how sorry they were. And they began to try to please God.

It had happened just as Jonah thought it would. Now God did not have to punish the people.

Jonah sat down outside the city and sulked.

It was very hot, so God made a plant with enormous leaves to grow near Jonah. Jonah enjoyed the shade.

But the next day the plant was dead.
There was no shade. Jonah was hot and
upset.

God said, 'Why are you so grumpy?'

Jonah said, 'I'm upset because this
plant is dead — and I'm angry about
Nineveh.'

God said, 'I made that plant, Jonah,
and I made the people of Nineveh. If you
are sorry for the plant, shouldn't I feel
sorry for the people? Be glad that they
are still alive to enjoy the life I have
given them.'

The Story Bible Series from Guideposts is made up of 50 individual stories for young readers, building up an understanding of the Bible as one story—God's story—a story for all time and all people.

The Old Testament story books tell the story of a great nation—God's chosen people, the Israelites—and God's love and care for them through good times and bad. The stories are about people who knew and trusted God. From this nation came one special person, Jesus Christ, sent by God to save all people everywhere.

The New Testament story books cover the life and teaching of God's Son, Jesus. The stories are about the people he met, what he did and what he said. Almost all we know about the life of Jesus is recorded in the four Gospels—Matthew, Mark, Luke and John. The word gospel means 'good news.'

The last four stories in this section are about the first Christians, who started to tell others the 'good news,' as Jesus had commanded them—a story which continues today all over the world.

The story of Jonah is one of the best known of all Bible stories. It has some important lessons to teach. As Jonah knew, God's love reaches out to people everywhere. After all, he is the one who made us. And although he cannot let evil continue unchecked, because he is just and good, what he wants is not to punish but to see people change their ways. He is ready to forgive those who are really sorry for the wrong they have done, and who want to make a new start.

Jonah found this hard to take, because he wanted to see God destroy the people of Nineveh. This was the capital city of the Assyrians, whose fierce armies invaded and laid waste too many countries. Surely they deserved to be punished?